The Legend of the Golden Cat

Written by Cas Lester

Illustrated by Adilson Farias

UNIVERSITY PRESS

Words to look out for ...

ambition (*noun*)
An ambition is something you want to do very much.

attentive (*adjective*)
listening or watching carefully

convey (*verb*)
conveys, conveying, conveyed
To convey someone or something is to take them somewhere.

devise (*verb*)
devises, devising, devised
To devise a plan or idea is to think it up.

incident (*noun*)
something that happens, usually something bad or strange

observe (*verb*)
observes, observing, observed
To observe someone or something is to watch them carefully.

reputation (*noun*)
what most people say or think about someone or something

scale (*noun*)
The scale of a map or model is its size compared to the real world, e.g. one centimetre representing one kilometre.

Chapter One

Once, in a kingdom far away, there lived a cat called Indigo. She was bold and smart and had a taste for adventure. She was also a little bit scruffy.

Indigo's best friend was a boy called Tyra. He worked in the palace, looking after the queen's cat, Ozzalino.

The queen's cat Ozzalino was treated like royalty. He ate out of golden dishes, and slept on a velvet cushion.

He spent all day eating, snoozing and lazing around …

… but Indigo wasn't jealous. She liked more action and adventure in her life. She wished she could eat as much as Ozzalino, though!

Ozzalino's favourite snoozing spot was beneath the Golden Cat statue.

This precious statue was made of solid gold. It was kept in the hallway of the palace.

Ozzalino liked to be fed underneath the statue. It made him feel important. He had his bed under it too!

There was a legend about the statue. The story said that the statue was protected by a giant cat who slept under the mountains.

People said that if anyone stole the statue, the giant cat would wake up. Then something terrible would happen to the thief.

As our story begins, Indigo hadn't eaten all day.

She watched Tyra carrying Ozzalino's bowl. It was full of delicious-looking food. Her stomach growled.

Indigo sneaked into the palace on soft, silent paws. She kept a sharp eye out for Ozzalino. He had a reputation for being bad at sharing.

There was no sign of Ozzalino, so she started eating from his bowl.

Your reputation is what most people say or think about you.

Suddenly, there was an ear-splitting yowl. Ozzalino leapt out from behind the statue.

'*Scruff-pots like you aren't allowed in here,*' he hissed. His tail shook furiously. '*Get out!*'

Indigo left at once. She didn't want to cause trouble for Tyra.

A short while later, Tyra slipped outside too. He had a small bowl of food for Indigo.

'Don't let Ozzalino see,' he whispered as he left.

Indigo purred to thank him and happily started to eat.

Then, suddenly, a shadow fell across her.

'Gotcha!' cried a voice. Indigo was shoved inside a smelly old sack.

'Let me out!' Indigo cried. Of course, the kidnappers heard only an angry howl.

Whoever had grabbed Indigo just laughed.

Then she was being bumped along. She could hear pounding hooves.

Indigo struggled desperately. *Where are they taking me?* she thought.

'We'll go straight to our den,' said a mean-sounding voice.
'The chief will be pleased.'

'Why does the chief want a cat?' asked another voice.

'She's <u>devised</u> a clever plan,' said the first voice. 'We can exchange the kidnapped kitty. We'll get the Statue of the Golden Cat without stealing it. The giant cat won't come after us!'

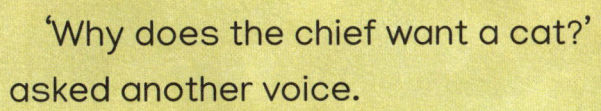

To <u>devise</u> a plan or idea is to think it up.

'Will they really give us a precious statue? Why would they want this scruffy old thing?' asked a deeper voice.

Who are you calling scruffy? Indigo thought crossly.

'Of course they will,' the first kidnapper replied. 'This is the queen's cat!'

Then Indigo realized the kidnappers' mistake. They thought she was the palace cat, Ozzalino!

Chapter Two

It was a long ride to the kidnappers' den. Indigo was getting all bumped and bruised.

Finally, she was let out of the sack. She was in a dark and gloomy wooden hut.

The kidnapping gang looked like a bumbling bunch to Indigo.

Only one of the kidnappers seemed to know what was going on.

That must be the chief, Indigo thought.

The chief looked tough. She had a fierce scowl on her face. She observed Indigo closely.

'That's not the palace cat!' she cried.

The rest of the gang shrank back in fear.

To observe someone or something is to watch them carefully.

One of them stammered, 'It must be! A servant was feeding it in the palace garden!'

'Huh! That's just a scruffy, flea-bitten old moggy,' snapped the chief.

How dare you – I do not have fleas! thought Indigo, scratching her ear.

She flicked her tail and gave the woman a cross hiss.

'Shove that cat back in the sack,' the chief said. 'Just get rid of her!'

The nearest kidnapper grabbed at Indigo. Indigo let out her claws – PING, PING-a-PING!

'Yeowch!' the kidnapper squealed, rubbing his hand. 'That really hurt!' The rest of the gang backed away.

Quick as a flash, Indigo leapt out of the window and ran.

Indigo raced along the road. Her paws pounded.

Suddenly, she heard the sound of horses' hooves. They were getting louder. The horses were catching her up.

She looked back for just a moment. It was the kidnappers! Hurriedly, Indigo shot up a tree. The gang rushed past beneath her.

Oh no! thought Indigo. *They're going to the palace to get Ozzalino! I must warn Tyra!*

She raced after the gang, but it was a long way back. The kidnappers were on horseback. They would get to the palace long before she did.

Sure enough, by the time Indigo got there, it was too late.

Ozzalino was gone.

Chapter Three

Tyra was sitting on the steps of the palace. He looked completely miserable. Indigo noticed he was clutching a piece of paper.

'Indigo, there you are!' he cried. 'I've been so worried. Ozzalino's been kidnapped! The kidnappers left this note. It says that they want the Statue of the Golden Cat!'

'I don't know what to do,' Tyra moaned. 'I can't leave Ozzalino with the kidnappers, but I can't steal the statue either. If I take it, the giant cat will wake up!'

Indigo was quiet and attentive. She looked at Tyra. They both knew the legend. Something terrible would happen to anyone who stole the statue.

If you are attentive, you are listening or watching carefully.

What would the giant cat do to us? thought Indigo fearfully.

Tyra looked scared. He was wondering the same thing.

Indigo knew what they had to do, though.

Indigo walked towards the statue, and nudged Ozzalino's empty bed. She gave a loud meow and looked back at Tyra with wide eyes.

Tyra understood. 'You're right, Indigo,' he said. 'You and I have to rescue Ozzalino.'

Tyra turned over the kidnappers' note. They'd drawn a map there. With a paw, Indigo patted at a large red 'X' on the map.

'I guess that's where we have to take the statue,' said Tyra. 'It's a very long way.'

We'll never rescue Ozzalino in time, thought Indigo. *The queen's sure to notice he's missing.*

Tyra's face suddenly lit up. 'This route goes along the road,' he said excitedly, 'but I see a shortcut!'

Tyra showed Indigo the shortcut on the map.

Indigo's eyes widened with alarm.

'All I have to do is get across the Raging River,' said Tyra. 'Then I go over the Horribly High Bridge. After that, I enter the Dangerously Deep Dark Jungle. Finally, I'll find the spot marked by that cross. How hard can it be?'

It sounds terribly risky to me, thought Indigo.

Tyra fetched his bag. Taking a deep breath, he picked up the Golden Cat statue and put it in the bag.

'You stay here,' he told Indigo. 'I don't want you to get hurt.'

Indigo meowed crossly and pushed up against Tyra's legs. She wouldn't let him face the dangerous journey alone.

In the end, they went together. Tyra followed the map. Indigo kept a careful look out for giant cats.

Soon, Tyra and Indigo got to the Raging River.

There was no bridge. They couldn't see a boat, either. There was nothing to convey them across the river.

Then they spotted a line of stepping stones.

Indigo jumped on to the first one – and yowled! It was as slippery as ice. She had nearly fallen into the river!

To convey someone or something is to take them somewhere.

Carefully, they made it halfway across.

Then, suddenly, an alligator leapt up! It snapped its enormous jaws and nearly took off Indigo's whiskers!

Indigo let out her claws – PING, PING-a-PING! Then she gave the alligator a sharp scratch on the nose. It slunk away.

Tyra and Indigo dashed to the safety of the other bank.

Next, they had to cross the Horribly High Bridge.

Indigo gazed at it. The ropes were old and thin. Many slats were broken. It was a very long drop to the ground!

They crept cautiously on to the bridge. It wobbled wildly.

Then Tyra tripped – and dropped the bag with the statue!

Just in time, Indigo sank her claws into Tyra's tunic and he scrambled back up.

The bag hung from a thin, shaky branch below them.

Quickly, Tyra tied a loose slat to some rope. He hooked it on to the strap – just before the branch snapped!

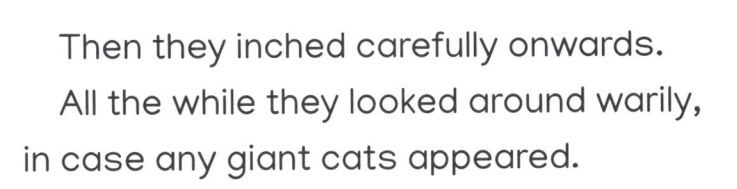

Then they inched carefully onwards.
All the while they looked around warily, in case any giant cats appeared.

Chapter Four

Finally, Tyra and Indigo were close to their goal: the 'X' on the map. It would be through the Dangerously Deep Dark Jungle.

The two friends plunged bravely in. The jungle was thick and creepy. They pushed their way through thick vines and giant ferns.

As they continued, Indigo kept hearing strange rustling noises. Something felt spooky. She drew closer to Tyra.

Could it be the cat from the legend? she thought. *Has it finally caught us?*

Indigo looked around fearfully. She couldn't see anything, except shadows.

Indigo and Tyra tried to work out their route. They had to find the place marked 'X'. The map's scale wasn't marked, though. They had no idea how far they had to go.

Soon Tyra became worried. It felt like they were going around in circles.

'Haven't we been past this tree already?' he wondered aloud. His voice was full of concern.

The scale of a map or model is its size compared to the real world, e.g. one centimetre representing one kilometre.

All the trees look the same to me, thought Indigo.

'We're lost,' groaned Tyra. 'Now we'll never rescue Ozzalino!'

Then Indigo had a clever idea. She flicked out her claws, PING, PING-a-PING! Then she scratched the bark of the nearest tree.

'Indigo, that's brilliant!' said Tyra. They made more marks on trees as they went on.

They seemed to walk for ages. Then, somehow, they found themselves back at the scratched trees.

'This is hopeless!' exclaimed Tyra. Indigo tried to encourage her friend not to give up. She meowed boldly.

'Which way now, then?' demanded Tyra miserably.

Indigo looked around her. *This way!* she decided, and confidently set off.

Tyra followed her. Then, all of a sudden, there was another horrible incident.

The ground gave way – and Tyra and Indigo fell into a hole!

They had walked right into a trap.

The kidnapping gang looked down at them, laughing.

'I think we might have found the 'X',' said Tyra gloomily.

An incident is something that happens, usually something bad or strange.

Chapter Five

The kidnappers dragged Tyra and Indigo back to their den.

Tyra immediately looked around for Ozzalino.

'Where's the queen's cat?' he demanded.

There was a faint yowl. It came from inside a large wicker basket.

'*I'm in here!*' Indigo heard Ozzalino call.

Tyra ducked out of the reach of the kidnappers. He rushed over to the basket. It was tied tightly shut with thick leather straps.

Tyra quickly undid the straps and set the cat free.

There was a rush of ginger fur as Ozzalino leapt out. He yowled furiously. His green eyes flashed with fury.

'Don't let them get away!' yelled the chief. She ran to the door and slammed it shut.

The kidnappers all rushed to do as they were told. One tried to seize Ozzalino. Ozzalino spat and lashed out with his claws, and the man jumped back.

Indigo was impressed to see Ozzalino being so fierce. He'd always seemed so lazy and spoilt.

'Where's the Statue of the Golden Cat?' demanded the chief.

One of the men handed her Tyra's bag. The chief snatched it eagerly.

'Now let us go!' said Tyra.

'No,' said the chief.

'What? That was the deal!' cried Tyra hotly.

'Yes, but now we've got the gold statue, *and* the queen's cat, *and* two prisoners,' sneered the chief.

Indigo was outraged. They'd been cheated!

Suddenly there was a deep, grumbling sound – as if a mountain was moving.

'It's an earthquake!' cried the kidnappers.

'It's only thunder!' sneered their chief. 'What a bunch of scaredy-cats!'

'How rude!' hissed Ozzalino. *'I'm not afraid of thunder!'*

Indigo wasn't sure it was thunder at all …

The building shuddered. It felt like the ground was being shaken.

Suddenly, a gleaming eye appeared at the window.

It was the eye of an enormous stone cat.

'It's the legend!' cried Tyra. 'The giant cat has woken up!'

Everyone stared at the huge cat in wonder. Indigo crouched nervously.

The giant cat flattened its ears. It hissed, showing its huge teeth.

Instantly, the kidnappers flung open the door and ran away. They were never seen again.

The giant cat slid its massive paw in through the doorway. It stuck its claws into Tyra's bag and dragged it outside.

Indigo peered out through the window. The enormous cat had lain down with the statue between its front paws. It was watching the doorway.

What is it going to do now? wondered Indigo anxiously.

'It's guarding the door,' exclaimed Tyra. 'We're trapped!'

Indigo was devising a plan. She would explain everything.

To devise a plan or idea is to think it up.

Plucking up her courage, Indigo walked bravely outside. The stone cat turned its huge eyes on her. Indigo felt as if it could see inside her and hear her thoughts. She was filled with wonder.

Indigo tried talking to the giant cat. *'We only stole the statue to rescue Ozzalino,'* she explained. *'He'd been kidnapped.'*

The giant cat was very attentive. It seemed to understand her.

If you are attentive, you are listening or watching carefully.

When she finished her tale, Indigo made a promise. *'We'll take the statue back to the palace,'* she said.

The gigantic cat blinked slowly. Then it nodded.

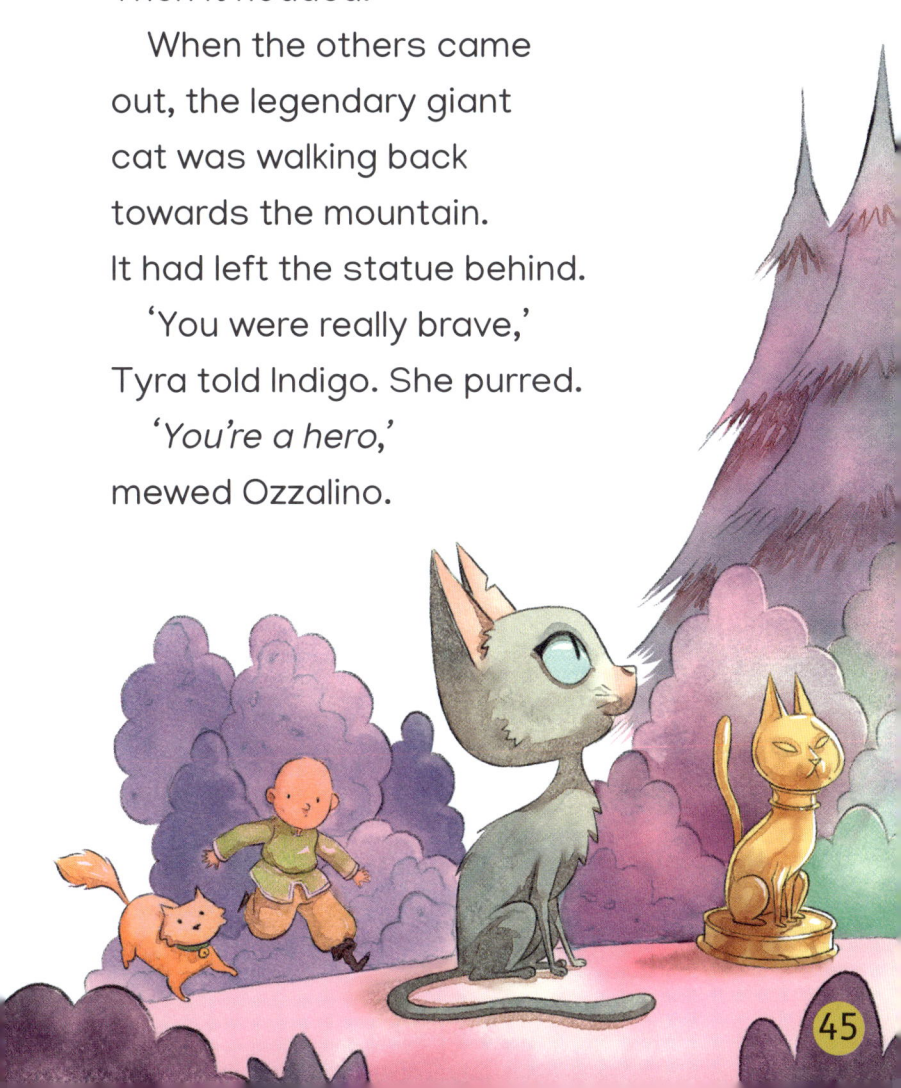

When the others came out, the legendary giant cat was walking back towards the mountain. It had left the statue behind.

'You were really brave,' Tyra told Indigo. She purred.

'You're a hero,' mewed Ozzalino.

Tyra picked up his bag. 'Come on,' he said. 'Let's get back quickly. The queen mustn't find out that Ozzalino's gone!'

They hurried back to the palace, taking the shortcut again. This time, they knew how to face its dangers.

At last, they made it. The queen had only just spotted Ozzalino's empty bed!

'Indigo, I'll tell the queen what you did,' Tyra said.

Indigo purred modestly.

'I'm sorry I called you a scruff-pot, Indigo,' meowed Ozzalino. *'I won't chase you out of the palace again. If you like, you can live here!'*

Indigo had no ambition to be a pampered royal cat. She didn't want to laze around all day.

An ambition is something you want to do very much.

'*Thank you, but I like more adventure in my life!*' she mewed.

She did agree to one thing, though.

Now, Indigo gets an enormous dish of food every single day.

Tyra puts it next to Ozzalino's – right under the Statue of the Golden Cat.